METHAMPHETAMINES
AFFECTING LIVES

BY K. A. ARTANNE

MOMENTUM

Published by The Child's World®
1980 Lookout Drive • Mankato, MN 56003-1705
800-599-READ • www.childsworld.com

Photographs ©: Kaesler Media/Shutterstock
Images, cover, 1; Red Line Editorial, 5; Andrey
Popov/iStockphoto, 6; Raman Mistsechka/
iStockphoto, 9; Shutterstock Images, 10, 12,
18, 28; Anastasika Yar/Shutterstock Images,
15; ESB Professional/Shutterstock Images, 16;
Photographee.eu/Shutterstock Images, 21;
iStockphoto, 22, 23, 27; Daniel Basaldua Rubio/
iStockphoto, 24

ISBN 9781503844957 (Reinforced Library Binding)
ISBN 9781503846456 (Portable Document Format)
ISBN 9781503847644 (Online Multi-user eBook)
LCCN 2019957969

Printed in the United States of America

Some names and details have been changed
throughout this book to protect privacy.

CONTENTS

MOMENTUM

FAST FACTS

What They Are

► Methamphetamines, or meth, are drugs that speed up the body's system. They are also called bikers coffee, chalk, crank, crystal, ice, shards, and speed.

How They're Used

► Methamphetamines are originally made as a powder. The powder can be swallowed. It can also be snorted, or sniffed, through the nose.

► Meth can be mixed with liquid and **injected** into the body with a needle.

► Crystal meth looks like shards of glass, or crystal, and is smoked in a glass pipe.

Physical Effects

► Meth raises a person's heart rate, body temperature, and blood pressure.

► Other effects can include extra energy, itchiness, and loss of teeth.

► High doses of meth may result in death from a heart attack or stroke.

Meth Use by Age

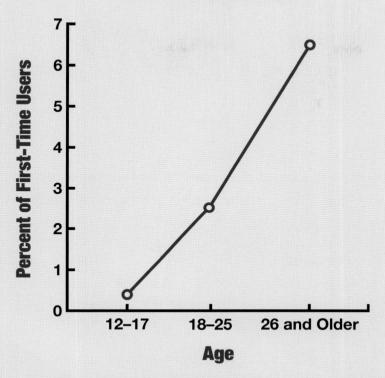

"Methamphetamine." *National Institute on Drug Abuse*, 2018, drugabuse.gov. Accessed 9 Dec. 2019.

A 2018 national survey found that less than 1 percent of kids under 18 years old have tried meth. About 6.5 percent of adults ages 26 and older have tried meth.

Mental Effects

► Meth leads to an intense wave of good feelings called **euphoria**. Euphoric feelings can last up to 12 hours.

► Some people experience anxiety and paranoia. Meth also causes some people to **hallucinate** or become violent.

CHAPTER ONE

BECOMING DEPENDENT

Taylor spun around on the dance floor. His heart beat fast and the music was loud in his ears. Taylor wiped the sweat from his forehead. It was time for a break. He and his friend Greg left the dance floor and walked outside to Greg's car. Once they sat down, Greg pulled a bag of white powder out of his glove compartment. Taylor knew it was drugs, but he didn't know what kind. Greg lined up the powder on an old CD case. Then, he snorted it through a plastic straw. Greg told Taylor it was speed. He asked Taylor if he wanted to try some.

Taylor wasn't sure he should. He knew that taking drugs could be very dangerous because they are **addictive**. But he also knew he wanted to keep dancing and wanted more energy. He decided to give the drug a try. Taylor immediately felt a burst of energy. Taylor later learned that speed was a nickname for meth.

◀ **Someone may form a line of powdered meth and then snort it through a straw or rolled-up dollar bill.**

He'd heard meth was a dangerous drug, but he still wanted more. He wanted the euphoric feeling he got when he tried it in Greg's car. Taylor called Greg and asked for more of the drug. Soon, it felt impossible to stop.

Taylor started snorting meth so often it became a part of his morning routine. One morning, he reached for the plastic bag he kept in the bathroom cabinet. He stored his meth inside of it. But when Taylor opened the bag, he saw it was empty. Taylor immediately felt anxious. He didn't know how to feel good without meth. His daily use had made him **dependent** on it.

Taylor looked in the mirror. He felt scared. He barely recognized himself. He'd lost a lot of weight and had dark bags under his eyes. He didn't know how this had happened. He also didn't know how to make his **cravings** stop.

That morning, Taylor realized something needed to change. Soon after, he checked himself into a **rehabilitation**, or rehab, program. For three months, he shared a room with three other men who were also struggling with addiction. Their rehab was very structured. The staff at the recovery center told him when to eat and sleep. They also told him when he needed to go to therapy. In therapy, Taylor talked with professionals who helped him to better control his addiction. It was hard for Taylor.

Meth use can change someone's appearance. ▶

▲ By sharing the stories of their addiction, people can warn others about the dangers of meth.

But over time, Taylor found some answers to his questions. He began to understand what it meant to be addicted to meth.

Taylor learned that addiction is a disease. He also learned that the areas of his brain involved with decision-making didn't work as well when he was on the drug. Though Taylor had been doing things that hurt himself and others, he hadn't been able to stop craving the drug. Rehab helped Taylor stop using drugs.

After Taylor left rehab, he became a writer and educator. He used his experiences to teach others about the dangers of drug use. Before that night in the car with Greg, Taylor had never heard of meth. Now, he wanted to make sure that what happened to him didn't happen to someone else.

METH LABS

Meth is dangerous not only for humans, but for the planet, too. It is illegal to cook meth. Some labs where people cook meth have been found in remote areas of natural forests in the United States. This is very bad for the environment. Cooking meth produces a lot of waste. Much of this waste is poisonous and can easily catch fire. Even when a meth lab has closed down, dangerous chemicals remain in the environment.

CHAPTER TWO

HURTING FAMILY RELATIONSHIPS

John walked through the cafeteria. It was his first day volunteering at his sister Hannah's elementary school. He waved when he saw her. Hannah grinned. As Hannah ran toward him, John thought about all the times his meth addiction had hurt her. There was the time he'd stolen money from her piggy bank so he could buy drugs. He had also been arrested in the front yard of their home. Hannah had burst into tears at the sight of her big brother in handcuffs. But John was **sober** now. He was determined not to **relapse**. He never wanted to hurt Hannah again.

After John returned home from volunteering, he got a phone call with some bad news. One of John's friends had died. John couldn't handle the sadness of losing his friend. He relapsed and smoked meth, because he thought it would make him feel better.

◄ **When someone feels sad or depressed, he or she may be more likely to relapse.**

But that only helped for a short time. When the euphoria wore off, John was ashamed. Even though he knew that relapses were common for people with addiction, he felt like he had failed.

John knew his parents would be angry. He didn't want to see their disappointed faces. He moved away from home. Before John left, he stole a coin collection that had once belonged to his grandfather. He knew he would need more money to pay for meth.

When John's parents realized he had relapsed, they stopped letting him see Hannah. His parents said he had hurt her too much. John was crushed. He knew they were right. But he also wanted to be a part of his sister's life.

John decided to enter a rehabilitation program. It wasn't his first time in rehab. But this time, he wasn't just getting help for himself. He was getting help so he could see Hannah.

The rehabilitation program helped John with his cravings. When it was over, John joined a support group for people with addiction. He and other members of his support group sat in a circle and talked about how meth had impacted their lives. Many of them had broken relationships with friends and family.

After a few months, John sent an email to his dad. He and his dad began communicating through email a few times a week.

Someone who cannot afford meth ▶ might steal to pay for the drug.

▲ Support groups at treatment centers
can make people feel less alone.

But his dad still wouldn't let John talk to Hannah. Two years passed, and John stayed sober with the help of his support group and family. He found a job and moved into a new apartment. He made new friends at work, so he wouldn't fall into the habit of hanging out with his friends who did drugs. He knew being around meth would make his cravings worse.

Finally, John's parents told him he could talk to Hannah. But John was worried. He thought Hannah might hate him. But Hannah was excited to see John. She forgave him. John couldn't believe it. He started volunteering at Hannah's school again. He and Hannah saw movies together and went to the park. Finally, John was the big brother he'd always wanted to be.

GETTING HELP

If someone is struggling with addiction, it's important to get help. Anyone should call 911 in a life-threatening emergency. For non-immediate help, the Substance Abuse and Mental Health Services Administration (SAMHSA) has a free, confidential, 24/7 National Helpline. The service directs callers to help in their area. The helpline can be reached at 1-800-662-HELP (4357). SAMHSA also has an online treatment locator available at https://findtreatment.samhsa.gov

CHAPTER THREE

A MOTHER'S ADDICTION

Gayle stood in the doorway of her daughter Melissa's house. Gayle's eyes filled with tears. Dishes caked with food lay on the floor. Dirty clothes were heaped in piles. It smelled like urine. Gayle's three grandchildren sat in the dirty living room, watching television. They looked like they needed a bath. The youngest child seemed to have been wearing the same diaper for several days.

Gayle walked inside as Melissa entered the room. She had open sores all over her body. Gayle knew immediately what it meant. Melissa had been hallucinating again. Under the influence of meth, Melissa often thought that bugs were crawling under her skin. She had picked at her skin so badly that the wounds had become infected.

◄ **People who are addicted to meth may find it hard to take care of their house.**

Melissa asked if Gayle could take the children. Melissa had learned that if the kids didn't find a new place to live, they would be taken from her by Child Protective Services, a government service that makes sure children are in a safe home. Melissa told Gayle that she sometimes left her drugs on the kitchen table or near the bathroom sink. She feared the kids would get into them. But Melissa didn't know how to stop using the drugs.

Gayle knew she had to do something. She called her husband, Mark, so they could talk about the situation. They loved their grandchildren and knew they were not safe with Melissa. They decided they would take care of Melissa's kids. Gayle buckled the children in her car and drove them to her house. She and Mark became foster parents to Melissa's three children. This meant that they supported and raised the children, but they did not adopt them.

Gayle and Mark traded their small car for a minivan. They moved into a larger home. That way, the kids would have more space. Gayle also set up appointments with doctors and dentists. Melissa had not taken care of her kids' health. The children talked with therapists, or professionals who helped with mental and emotional problems. This allowed the kids to discuss the scary experiences they'd had with Melissa. Before moving in with Gayle, the kids often didn't have clean clothes or food to eat.

▲ Someone on meth may have scary hallucinations.

▲ **Talking to a therapist about a parent's addiction can help some children feel better.**

They'd even been left with strangers who sometimes didn't know how to properly care for them.

While Gayle bought toys and clothes for the children, Melissa continued to use drugs. She'd built up a **tolerance**, so that she needed more and more meth to feel euphoria. To pay for the drugs, Melissa stole from her family, taking jewelry and money. She barely called to check in on her children.

Melissa's drug use was painful for Gayle. She missed the daughter she knew—the girl who had once earned good grades in school and had been the star player of the volleyball team.

▲ **Meth addiction can lead to damaged relationships.**

Gayle tried to check Melissa into rehab, but Melissa refused.
Gayle knew she could not help her daughter if Melissa did not
want to get better. The only way Gayle could help was to take
care of her grandchildren. She just hoped that someday, they
could have a good relationship with their mother as well.

CHAPTER FOUR

GOING TO PRISON

Breanna sat in her classmate's basement. People chattered in different corners of the room and music played loudly from speakers. Her leg bounced up and down as she looked around nervously. Breanna had just moved to town and she didn't know anyone very well. She had come to the party to make friends. No one had talked to her yet. But soon, someone passed her a pipe. The pipe looked like a glass tube with a ball on the end of it. Breanna peered inside of the pipe. It looked like there were shards of crystal inside of it. Breanna immediately recognized that the shards were meth.

Both of Breanna's parents were addicted to meth. They had gone through patterns of using meth and relapsing. A few years ago, her parents' drug use had caused the family to become homeless. Her parents had spent all of their money on meth.

◄ **Some people may smoke meth out of a glass pipe.**

They couldn't afford to pay for their house. Breanna and her family had to sleep on park benches. Two years ago, her father had almost died from using too much meth at one time.

At the party, Breanna knew she should turn down the meth pipe. The drug had caused her family many problems. She'd promised herself she would never try it. But Breanna desperately wanted to make friends. She thought smoking meth would help her fit in. Breanna told herself she would do it just this once and then never again. She didn't want to get addicted, like her parents were. Breanna felt the drug's effects within minutes. She loved the euphoric feeling. It made her feel as powerful as a superhero.

Even though Breanna said she wouldn't, she continued to do meth after the party. Then she started skipping school. Her grades worsened. Breanna had always wanted to be a veterinarian or a preschool teacher. But now the opportunity was slipping through her fingers. When it was time to make a decision about college, Breanna decided not to go.

One day, Breanna was riding in a car with her friends. The driver was speeding. A police car pulled up behind them and turned on its blue and red lights. They were getting pulled over. Breanna looked around at all of the drugs in the car. Breanna's friends shoved their drugs and pipes into Breanna's purse.

▲ **People who struggle with addiction may spend all of their money on drugs. They might not be able to afford a home and become homeless.**

Breanna was too scared to stop them. She just hoped the police wouldn't notice.

The officer knocked on the driver's window. Her friend rolled the window down and the officer looked inside the car. He looked into her friend's eyes. Then, his eyes drifted to Breanna's seat.

▲ Using meth is illegal. People may go to
jail if they are caught using it.

Her purse sat open beside her. The drugs were in plain view. The officer arrested Breanna. Since Breanna carried a large amount of meth, she could go to jail for five years.

Breanna was devastated. She knew it was hard for people with drug charges to work in certain professions. Breanna would probably never get to be a vet or a preschool teacher.

After Breanna got out of jail, she found reasons to be thankful that she had been arrested. Going to jail had made her realize she could have died from using too much meth. Now, Breanna had a future without meth. After two years of being sober, Breanna decided to become a sponsor. As a sponsor, she helped keep people with addictions from relapsing. Breanna made friends with the people she sponsored. She finally felt like she belonged.

THINK ABOUT IT

► Why would someone continue using meth if it harms their body and mind?
► How can using meth impact a person's future?
► What would you tell someone who wants to try meth just one time?

GLOSSARY

addictive (uh-DIK-tiv): An addictive substance makes people want to keep using it after they begin taking it. Meth is an addictive drug.

cravings (KRAY-vingz): Cravings are uncontrollable desires to have something. People may experience meth cravings if the drug is difficult for them to resist.

dependent (di-PEN-duhnt): A person who is dependent on a drug feels a physical need to keep taking it. People who are dependent on drugs often need medical help to stop using them.

euphoria (you-FOR-ee-uh): Euphoria is an intense feeling of happiness. Meth produces a sense of euphoria.

hallucinate (huh-LOO-suh-nayt): If someone sees, smells, or hears something that's not there, they have started to hallucinate. People who use meth may hallucinate.

injected (in-JEK-tid): When something is injected, it is put into someone's body using a needle. People can harm their blood vessels when they have injected meth.

rehabilitation (ree-uh-bil-uh-TAY-shun): Drug rehabilitation is a type of treatment for drug abuse. Most rehabilitation centers have strict rules for patients.

relapse (REE-laps): Relapse occurs when a person who has an addiction had stopped using the drug, but then starts using again. He experienced a relapse when he used meth after a hard day.

sober (SOH-bur): A person who is sober is no longer using drugs or alcohol. Staying sober after rehab can be very difficult.

tolerance (TOL-ur-uhnss): Someone who uses drugs often builds up a tolerance and has to use more of a drug to feel its effects. She had a high meth tolerance.

TO LEARN MORE

BOOKS

Alexander, Richard. *What's Drug Abuse?*
New York, NY: KidHaven Publishing, 2019.

Perritano, John. *Stimulants: Meth, Cocaine, and Amphetamines*. Broomall, PA: Mason Crest, 2017.

Sheff, David. *High: Everything You Want to Know about Drugs, Alcohol, and Addiction*. Boston, MA: Houghton Mifflin Harcourt, 2018.

WEBSITES

Visit our website for links about addiction to methamphetamines: **childsworld.com/links**

Note to Parents, Teachers, and Librarians: We routinely verify our Web links to make sure they are safe and active sites. So encourage your readers to check them out!

SELECTED BIBLIOGRAPHY

"Dangers of Meth Labs." *U.S. Forest Service*, n.d., fs.fed.us. Accessed 17 Dec. 2019.

"Meth Mouth and Crank Bugs: Meth-a-morphosis." *National Institute on Drug Abuse for Teens*, 11 Jan. 2010, teens.drugabuse.gov. Accessed 17 Dec. 2019.

"Methamphetamine." *National Institute on Drug Abuse*, 16 Oct. 2019, drugabuse.gov. Accessed 17 Dec. 2019.

INDEX

ABOUT THE AUTHOR

K. A. Artanne writes instructional materials, short stories, and books for children. A former health and human services professional, she is passionate about bringing awareness to social issues. K. A. is now a youth services librarian in Ohio. She surrounds herself with books, whether it's reading them, writing them, or recommending them to children and teens at the library.